The Cup Of Humanity
Okakura Kakuzo : Tea And Life
Quotes With Ikebana And Other Illustrations

Text and images are the property of the artist
credited herein. © 2011
CTG Publishing and Melanie Paquette Widmann

Front Cover Image:
A young lady binding her poem to the branch of a
cherry tree. E 1431-98.

ISBN-13: 978-1463580285
ISBN-10: 1463580282

The Cup Of Humanity

Okakura Kakuzo : Tea And Life
Quotes With Ikebana And Other Illustrations

Dedicated to
P.H. Paquette, Ph.D. and Suzan Schmekel

About Okakura Tenshin Kakuzo
From the forward of "The Awakening of Japan"

Okakura Kakuzo was born in Japan in 1863. Okakura graduated (1880) from Tokyo Imperial University. Soon thereafter he met Ernest Fenollosa who become the preeminent voice in defending Japan's traditional art forms against the drive to modernization and westernization of the early Meiji Restoration.

Under his influence Okakura worked toward reeducating the Japanese people to appreciate their own cultural heritage. He was one of the principal founders of the Tokyo Fine Arts School, opened in 1887. In 1898 Okakura was ousted from the school in an administrative struggle. He next established the Nippon Bijutsu-in (Japan Academy of Fine Arts) with the help of such followers as Hishida Shunso and Yokoyama Taikan.

A frequent traveler abroad, at the turn of the century Okakura became curator of the Oriental art division of the Boston Museum of Fine Arts. Many of his works, such as The Ideals of the East (1903), The Awakening of Japan (1904), and The Book of Tea (1906), were written in English in order to spread abroad his ideas.

A Labour Of Love
Print By Toshikata

Page 8

He only who has lived with the beautiful
can die beautifully.

Perfection is everywhere if we only choose to recognise it.

Hide yourself under a bushel quickly, for if your real usefulness were known to the world you would soon be knocked down to the highest bidder by the public auctioneer. Why do men and women like to advertise themselves so much?

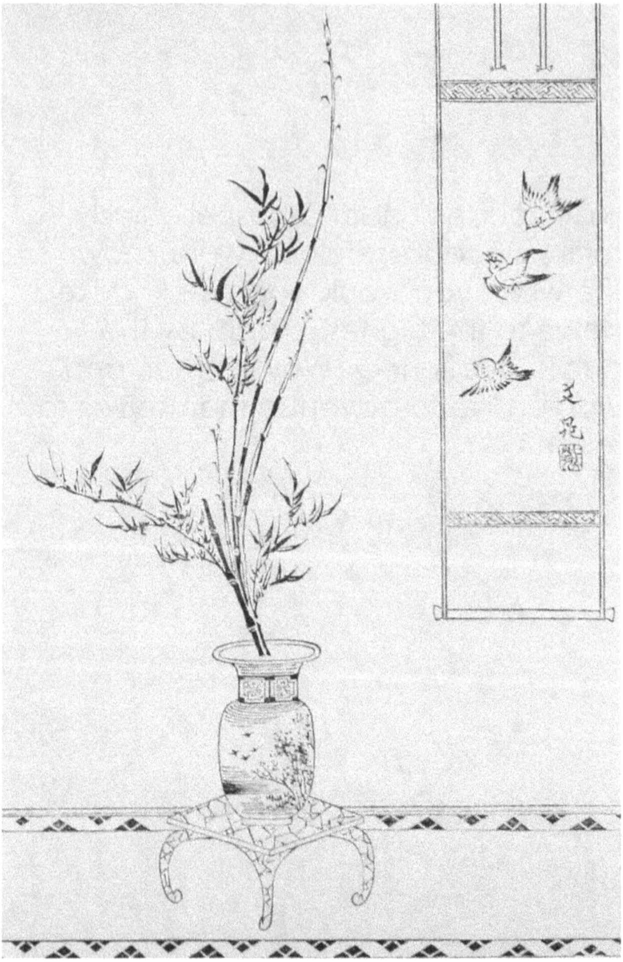

Arrangement of bamboo in standing porcelain vase, in front of picture of sparrows.

Those who cannot feel the littleness
of great things in themselves are apt
overlook the greatness of little things in
others.

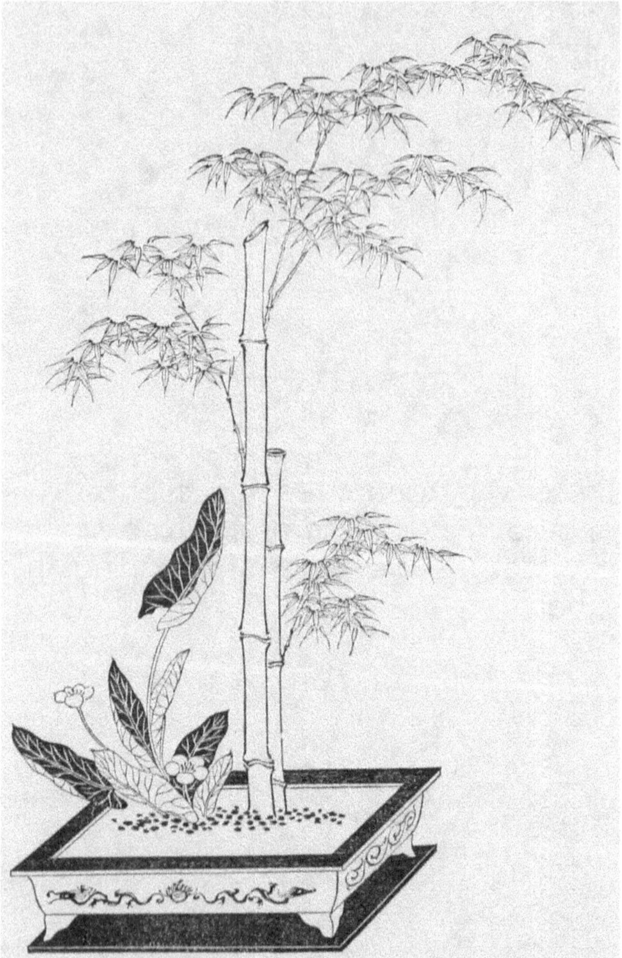

Arrangement of bamboo and nuphar
japonicum.

His works may be nearer science, but are further from humanity. We have an old saying in Japan that a woman cannot love a man who is truly vain, for there is no crevice in his heart for love to enter and fill up. In art vanity is equally fatal to sympathetic feeling, whether on the part of the artist or the public.

Triple arrangement of white plum, narcissus, and chrysanthemum in a two story bamboo vase with three openings.

How can one be serious with the world
when the world itself is so ridiculous!

He who had made himself master of the art of living was the Real Man of the Taoist. At birth he enters the realm of dreams only to awaken to reality at death. He tempers his own brightness in order to merge himself into the obscurity of others.

Those of us who know not the secret of properly regulating our own existence on this tumultuous sea of foolish troubles which we call life are constantly in a state of misery while vainly trying to appear happy and contented. We stagger in the attempt to keep our moral equilibrium, and see forerunners of the tempest in every cloud that floats on the horizon. Yet there is joy and beauty in the roll of the billows as they sweep outward toward eternity. Why not enter into their spirit, or, like Liehtse, ride upon the hurricane itself?

Arrangement of cabbage plant in globular
on legged stand.

The heaven of modern humanity is indeed shattered in the Cyclopean struggle for wealth and power. The world is groping in the shadow of egotism and vulgarity. Knowledge is bought through a bad conscience, benevolence practised for the sake of utility. The East and West, like two dragons tossed in a sea of ferment, in vain strive to regain the jewel of life. We need a Niuka again to repair the grand devastation; we await the great Avatar. Meanwhile, let us have a sip of tea.

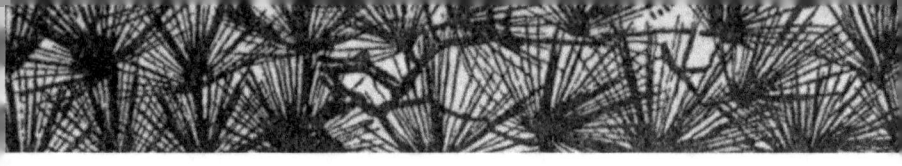

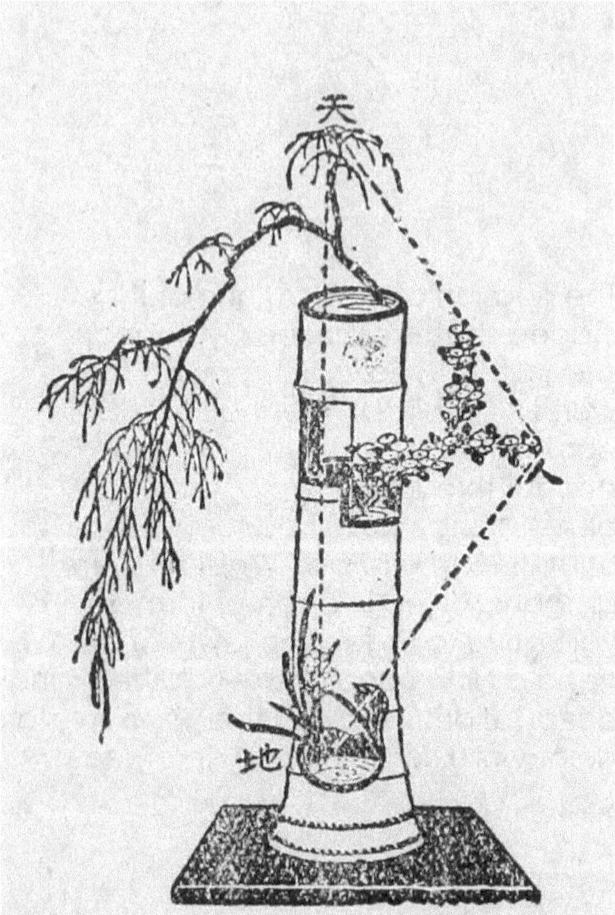

天

地

Arranging flowers from "Ikebana no tebiki".

The outsider may indeed wonder at this seeming much ado about nothing. What a tempest in a tea-cup! he will say. But when we consider how small after all the cup of human enjoyment is, how soon overflowed with tears, how easily drained to the dregs in our quenchless thirst for infinity, we shall not blame ourselves for making so much of the tea-cup.

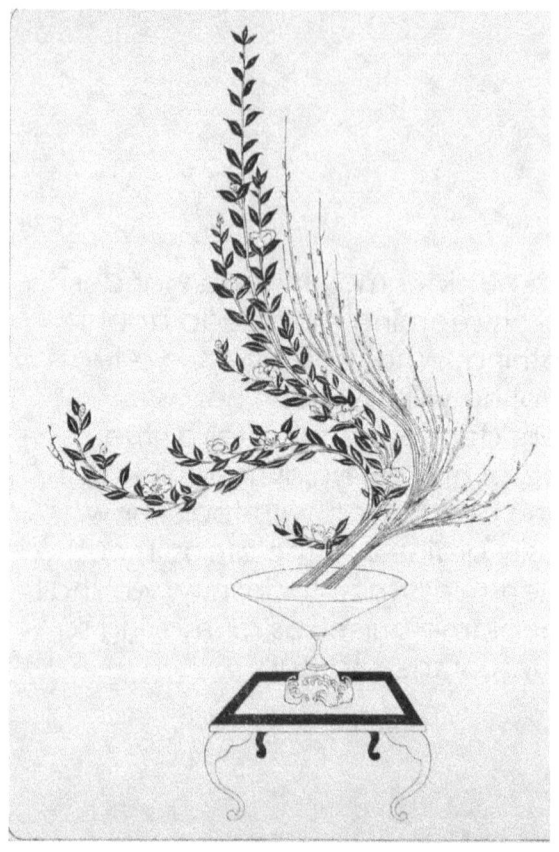

Arrangement of willow and camellia
sasanqua (sazankwa) in wide mouthed
bronze vase.

Tea began as a medicine and grew into a beverage.

The beverage soon became a
necessary of life—a taxable matter.

The beverage grew to be an excuse for the worship of purity and refinement, a sacred function at which the host and guest joined to produce for that occasion the utmost beatitude of the mundane. The tea-room was an oasis in the dreary waste of existence where weary travelers could meet to drink from the common spring of art appreciation.

Arrangement of weeping willow and
narcissus in wide-mouthed bronze vase.

A new meaning grew into the art of life. The tea began to be not a poetical pastime, but one of the methods of self realization. Wangyucheng eulogized tea as "flooding his soul like a direct appeal, that its delicate bitterness reminded him of the after-taste of a good counsel."

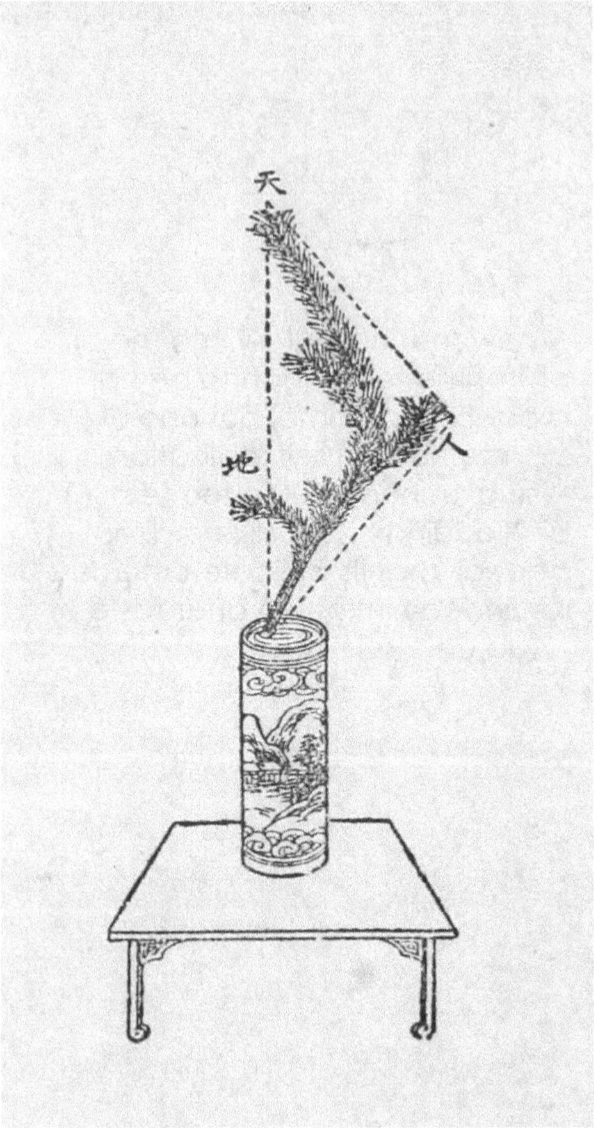

天

人

地

Arranging flowers from "Ikebana no tebiki".

Teaism is a cult founded on the
adoration of the beautiful among the
sordid facts of everyday existence.
It inculcates purity and harmony,
the mystery of mutual charity, the
romanticism of the social order.

壽獻金莖露歌飜玉樹塵

Combined arrangement of tecoma grandiflora (nozen kazura) in suspended crescent shaped vessel and calendula officinalis (kinsenkwa) in standing bronze vase.

Teaism. A worship of the Imperfect, as it is a tender attempt to accomplish something possible in this impossible thing we know as life.

Teaism is hygiene, for it enforces
cleanliness; it is economics, for it shows
comfort in simplicity rather than in
the complex and costly; it is moral
geometry, inasmuch as it defines our
sense of proportion to the universe.

Teaism is the art of concealing
beauty that you may discover it, of
suggesting what you dare not reveal.

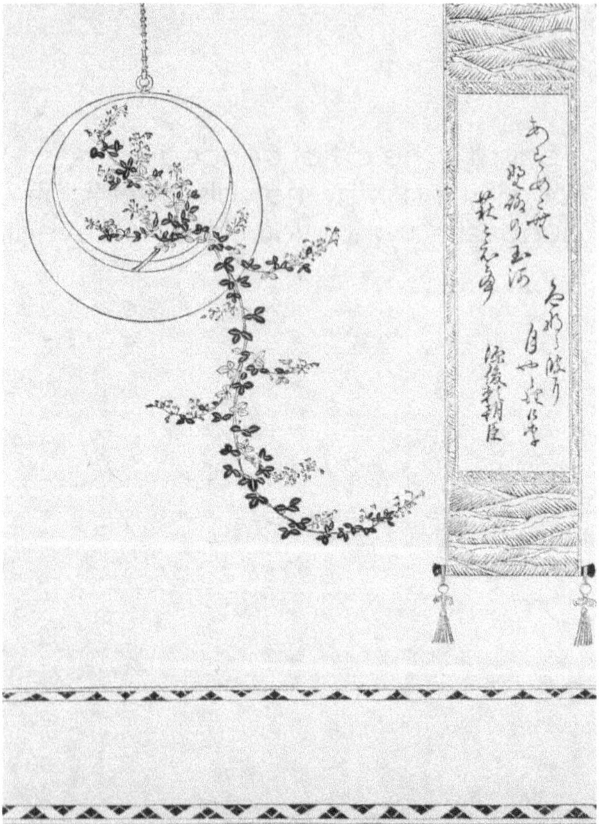

あさめくて
悲悩の玉河
萩ち右や

名れ流り
自此枝色や

深後判官

Arrangement of lespedeza (hagi) in
suspended crescent shaped vessel in front
of handing manuscript.

Teaism is the noble secret of laughing at yourself, calmly yet thoroughly, and is thus humour itself,—the smile of philosophy.

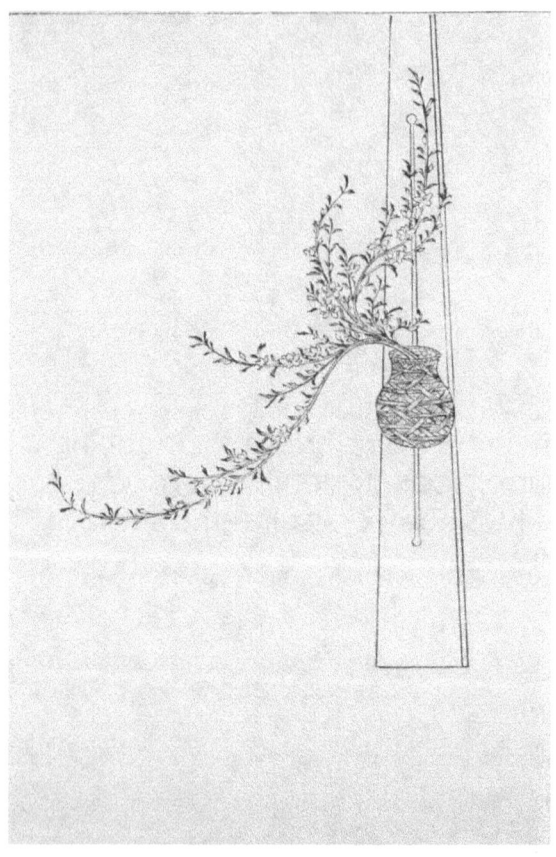

Arrangement of peach blossoms in hooked vase.

In our common parlance we speak of the man "with no tea " in him, when he is insusceptible to the seriocomic interests of the personal drama. Again we stigmatise the untamed aesthete who, regardless of the mundane tragedy, runs riot in the springtide of emancipated emotions, as one "with too much tea" in him.

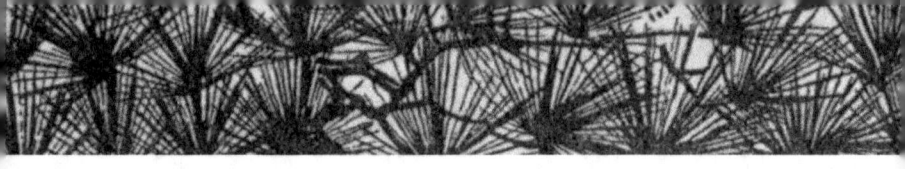

Arrangement of peach blossoms in a
standing flower-basket with the rosa indica.

Let us have a sip of tea. The afternoon glow is brightening the bamboos, the fountains are bubbling with delight, the soughing of the pines is heard in our kettle. Let us dream of evanescence, and linger in the beautiful foolishness of things.

There is a subtle charm in the taste of tea which makes it irresistible and capable of idealization. Western humourists were not slow to mingle the fragrance of their thought with its aroma. It has not the arrogance of wine, the self-consciousness of coffee, nor the simpering innocence of cocoa.

Tea is a work of art and needs a master hand to bring out its noblest qualities. We have good and bad tea, as we have good and bad paintings — generally the latter.

駒りある事がら 皇太后宮太夫
たち折山吹の
むら残をや 俊成
井出の玉川

Arrangement of kerria japonica in a
horse-tub.

There is no single recipe for making the perfect tea, as there are no rules for producing a Titian or a Sesson. Each preparation of the leaves has its individuality, its special affinity with water and heat, its hereditary memories to recall, its own method of telling a story. The truly beautiful must be always in it.

Arrangements of a simple five-lined composition with Narcissus.

15

The cake-tea which was boiled, the powdered-tea which was whipped, the leaf-tea which was steeped, mark the distinct emotional impulses of the Tang, the Sung, and the Ming dynasties of China. If we were inclined to borrow the much-abused terminology of art-classification, we might designate them respectively, the Classic, the Romantic, and the Naturalistic schools of tea.

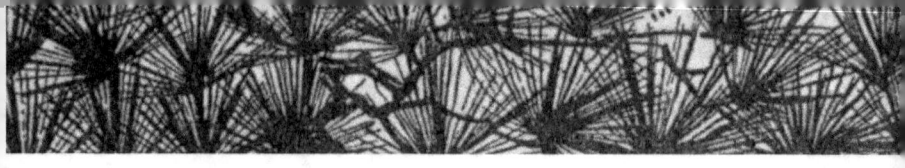

Arrangement of diantlius superbus
(nadeshiko) placed in a bronze vase.

Like Art, Tea has its periods and its schools. Its evolution may be roughly divided into three main stages: the Boiled Tea, the Whipped Tea, and the Steeped Tea. We moderns belong to the last school. These several methods of appreciating the beverage are indicative of the spirit of the age in which they prevailed.

It is interesting to observe in this connection the influence of tea on Chinese ceramics. The Celestial porcelain, as is well known, had its origin in an attempt to reproduce the exquisite shade of jade, resulting, in the Tang dynasty, in the blue glaze of the south, and the white glaze of the north. Luwuh considered the blue as the ideal color for the tea-cup, as it lent additional greenness to the beverage, whereas the white made it look pinkish and distasteful. It was because he used cake-tea. Later on, when the tea masters of Sung took to the powdered tea, they preferred heavy bowls of blue black and dark brown. The Mings, with their steeped tea, rejoiced in light ware of white porcelain.

There are three stages of boiling: the first boil is when the little bubbles like the eye of fishes swim on the surface; the second boil is when the bubbles are like crystal beads rolling in a fountain; the third boil is when the billows surge wildly in the kettle.

Arrangement of three convolvulus blossoms, placed in a standing vase on a high table.

It needed the genius of the Tang
dynasty to emancipate tea from
its crude state and lead to its final
idealization.

Arrangement of leaf-orchid in a hexagonal
bronze vase,

We classify too much and enjoy too little.

Arrangement of clematis in double well bucket display.

A Chinese critic complained many centuries ago, "People criticize a picture by their ear." It is this lack of genuine appreciation that is responsible for the pseudo-classic horrors that to-day greet us wherever we turn.

Liehihlai, a Sung poet, has sadly remarked that there were three most deplorable things in the world: the spoiling of fine youths through false education, the degradation of fine paintings through vulgar admiration, and the utter waste of fine tea through incompetent manipulation.

Life is an expression, our unconscious actions the constant betrayal of our innermost thought. Confucius said that "man hideth not." Perhaps we reveal ourselves too much in small things because we have so little of the great to conceal.

Arrangement of nuphar japonica with
seven leaves and two flowers.

The sympathetic communion of minds necessary for art appreciation must be based on mutual concession. The spectator must cultivate the proper attitude for receiving the message, as the artist must know how to impart it. The tea-master, Kobori-Enshiu, himself a daimyo, has left to us these memorable words: " Approach a great painting as thou wouldst approach a great prince." In order to understand a masterpiece, you must lay yourself low before it and await with bated breath its least utterance.

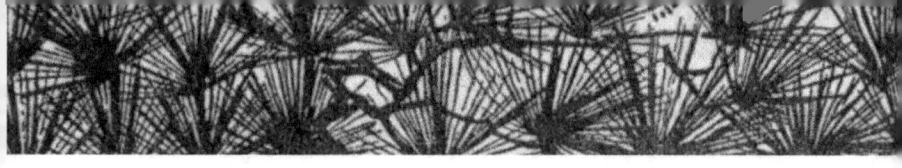

Arrangement of peonies with Irises.

We listen to the unspoken, we gaze upon the unseen. The master calls forth notes we know not of. Memories long forgotten all come back to us with a new significance. Hopes stifled by fear, yearnings that we dare not recognize, stand forth in new glory.

Arrangement of white peony (shiro
shakuyaku) of seven flowers in high bronze
vase.

Our mind is the canvas on which the artists lay their color; their pigments are our emotions; their chiaroscuro the light of joy, the shadow of sadness. The masterpiece is of ourselves, as we are of the masterpiece.

In leaving something unsaid the beholder is given a chance to complete the idea and thus a great masterpiece irresistibly rivets your attention until you seem to become actually a part of it. A vacuum is there for you to enter and fill up to the full measure of your aesthetic emotion.

The masters are immortal, for their loves and fears live in us over and over again. It is rather the soul than the hand, the man than the technique, which appeals to us,—the more human the call the deeper is our response. It is because of this secret understanding between the master and ourselves that in poetry or romance we suffer and rejoice with the hero and heroine.

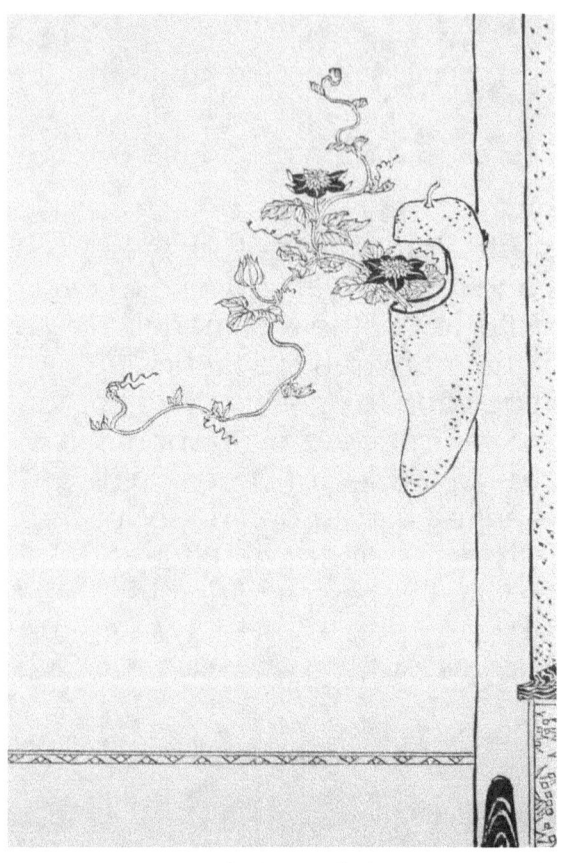

Arrangement of clematis in hooked display.

A master has always something to offer, while we go hungry solely because of our own lack of appreciation. To the sympathetic a masterpiece becomes a living reality towards which we feel drawn in bonds of comradeship.

Arrangement of Chrysanthemums in a triple design in a bamboo vase of three mouths, with fourteen blossoms in all.

We must remember, however, that art is of value only to the extent that it speaks to us. It might be a universal language if we ourselves were universal in our sympathies.

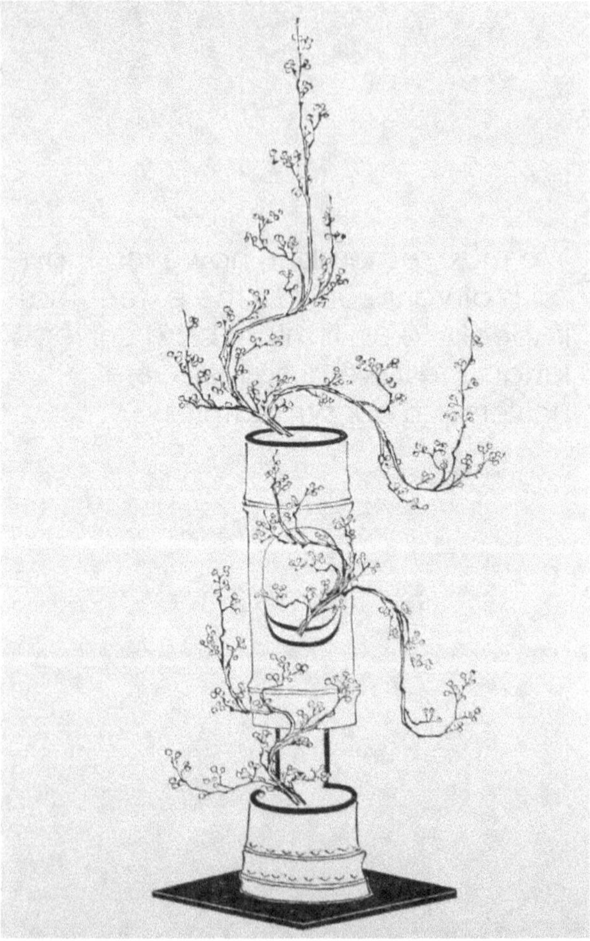

Arrangement of ilex sieboldi (ume-modori)
in three story bamboo vase.

It is true that with cultivation our sense of art appreciation broadens, and we become able to enjoy many hitherto unrecognized expressions of beauty. But, after all, we see only our own image in the universe,—our particular idiosyncrasies dictate the mode of our perceptions.

The art of to-day is that which really belongs to us: it is our own reflection. In condemning it we but condemn ourselves.

Art, to be fully appreciated, must be true to contemporaneous life. It is not that we should ignore the claims of posterity, but that we should seek to enjoy the present more. It is not that we should disregard the creations of the past, but that we should try to assimilate them into our consciousness. Slavish conformity to traditions and formulas fetters the expression of individuality in architecture.

Arrangement of species of pine (goyo no matsu) in standing bronze vase.

At the magic touch of the beautiful the secret chords of our being are awakened, we vibrate and thrill in response to its call. Mind speaks to mind. We listen to the unspoken, we gaze upon the unseen. The master calls forth notes we know not of. Memories long forgotten all come back to us with a new significance. Hopes stifled by fear, yearnings that we dare not recognize, stand forth in new glory.

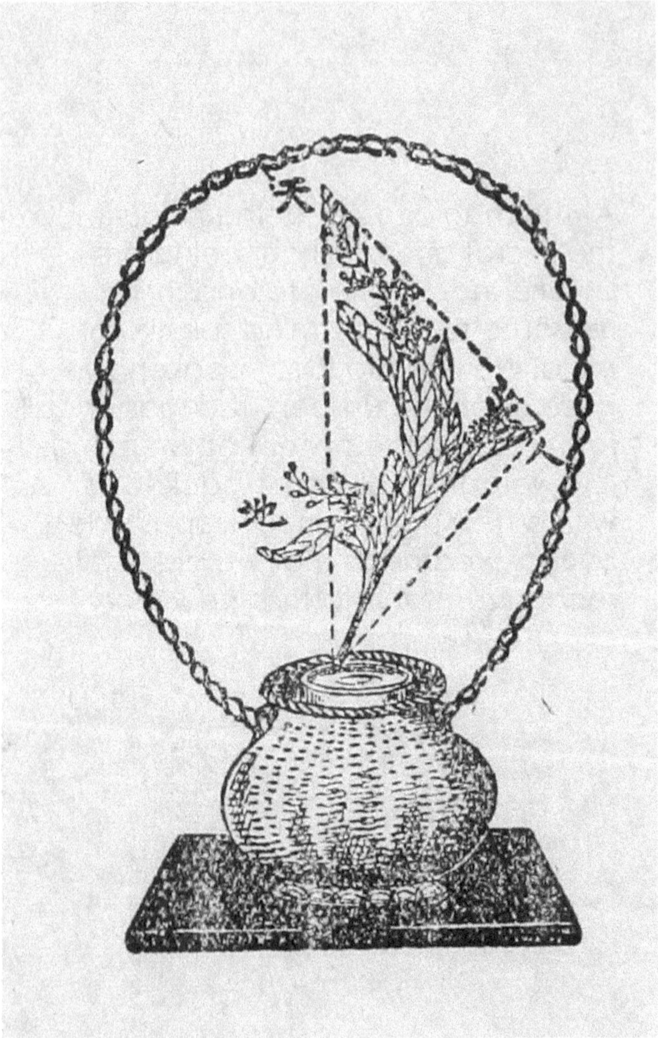

天

地

Arranging flowers from "Ikebana no tebiki".

Nothing is more hallowing than the union of kindred spirits in art. At the moment of meeting, the art lover transcends himself. At once he is and is not. He catches a glimpse of Infinity, but words cannot voice his delight, for the eye has no tongue. Freed from the fetters of matter, his spirit moves in the rhythm of things. It is thus that art becomes akin to religion and ennobles mankind. It is this which makes a masterpiece something sacred.

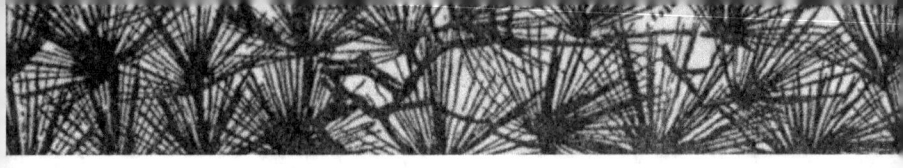

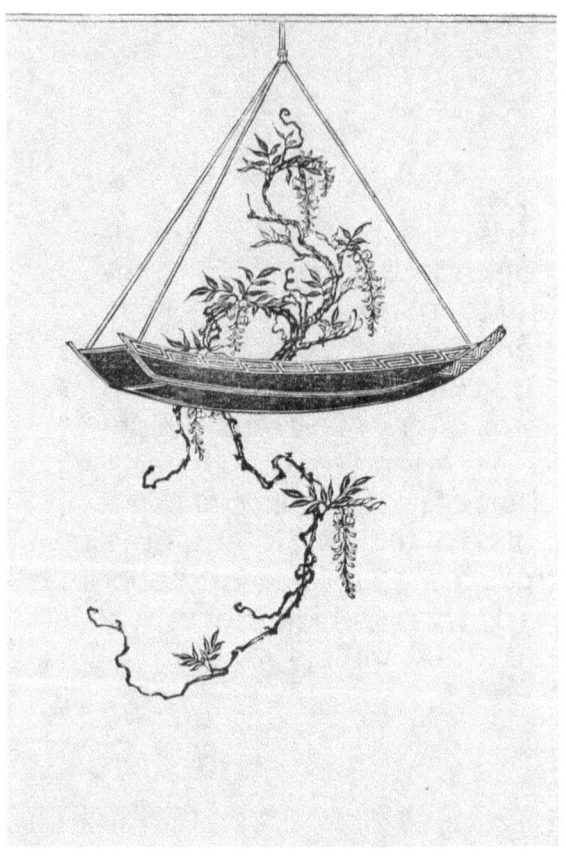

Arrangement of wistaria in suspended boat shaped vessel of bronze.

The tea-master strove to be something more than the artist,—art itself. It was the Zen of aestheticism.

When a tea-master has arranged a flower to his satisfaction he will place it on the Tokonoma, the place of honour in a Japanese room. Nothing else will be placed near it which might interfere with its effect, not even a painting, unless there be some special aesthetic reason for the combination. It rests there like an enthroned prince, and the guests or disciples on entering the room will salute it with a profound bow before making their addresses to the host.

The connection of Zennism with tea is proverbial.

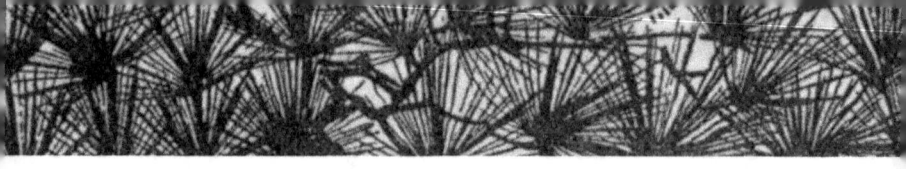

Arrangement of nandina domestica.

The whole ideal of Teaism is a result
of this Zen conception of greatness in
the smallest incidents of life.

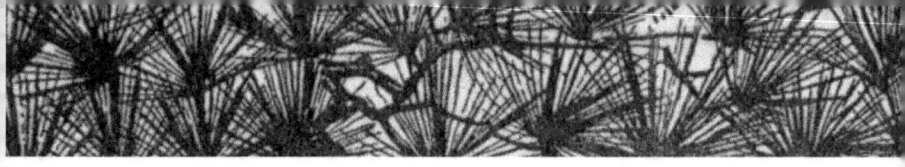

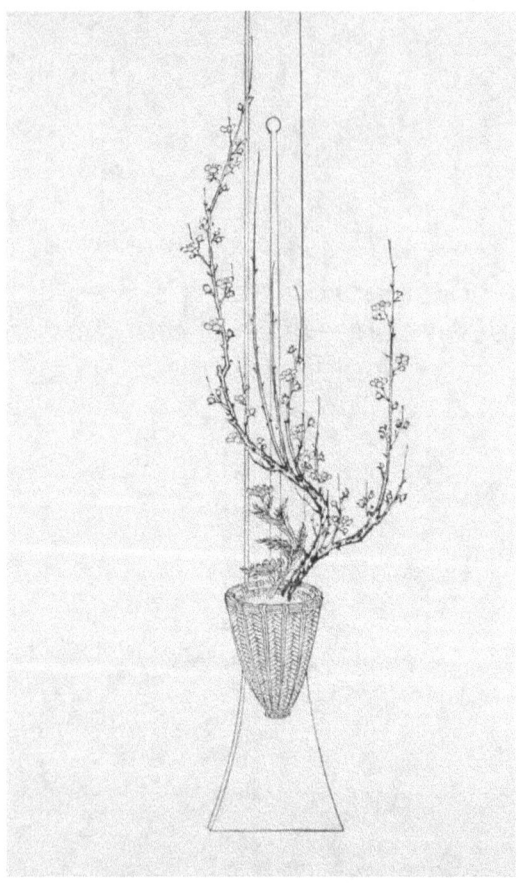

Arrangement of plum branch and Adonis amurensis (fukujuso) in basket, hooked against pillar tablet.

The tea-room (the Sukiya) does not pretend to be other than a mere cottage —a straw hut, as we call it.

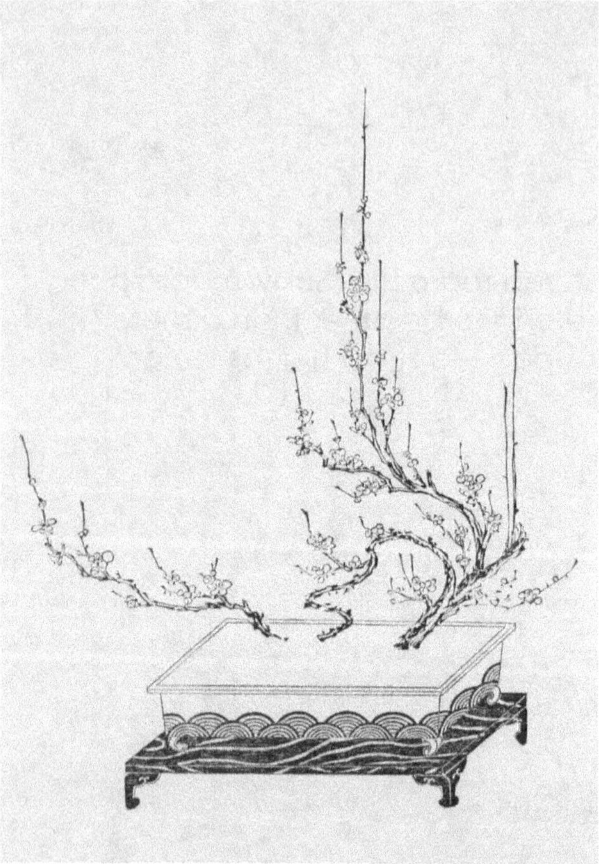

Arrangement of white plum in bronze basin,
with branch diving under the water.

The reality of a room, for instance, was to be found in the vacant space enclosed by the roof and walls, not in the roof and walls themselves. The usefulness of a water pitcher dwelt in the emptiness where water might be put, not in the form of the pitcher or the material of which it was made.

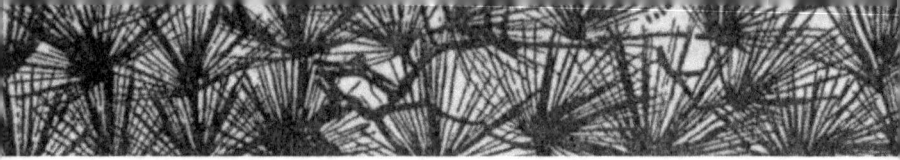

The tea-room is unimpressive in appearance. It is smaller than the smallest of Japanese houses, while the materials used in its construction are intended to give the suggestion of refined poverty. Yet we must remember that all this is the result of profound artistic forethought, and that the details have been worked out with care perhaps even greater than that expended on the building of the richest palaces and temples. A good tea-room is more costly than an ordinary mansion, for the selection of its materials, as well as its workmanship, requires immense care and precision.

The tea-room was an oasis in the dreary waste of existence where weary travelers could meet to drink from the common spring of art appreciation. The ceremony was an improvised drama whose plot was woven about the tea, the flowers, arid the paintings. Not a color to disturb the tone of the room, not a sound to mar the rhythm of things, not a gesture to obtrude on the harmony, not a word to break the unity of the surroundings, all movements to be performed simply and naturally—such were the aims of the tea-ceremony. And strangely enough it was often successful. A subtle philosophy lay behind it all. Teaism, was Taoism in disguise.

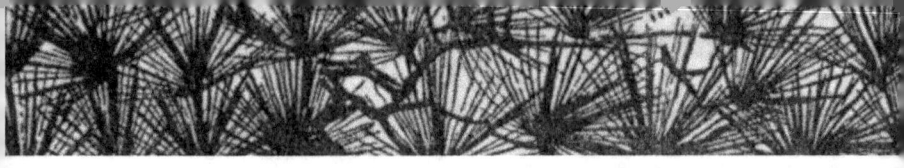

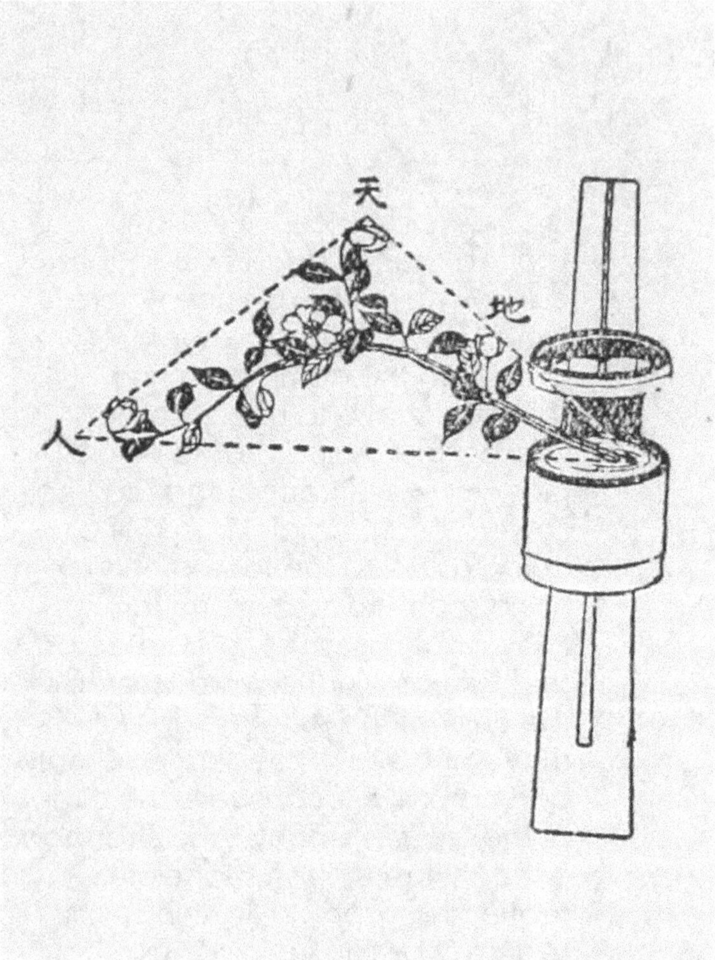

天

地

人

Arranging flowers from "Ikebana no tebiki".

Thus prepared the guest will silently approach the sanctuary, and, if a samurai, will leave his sword on the rack beneath the eaves, the tea-room being preeminently the house of peace.

Arrangement pine, plum and bamboo in
a saucer-shaped bronze vase forming the
floral triad called sho-chiku-bai.

Then he will bend low and creep into the room through a small door not more than three feet in height. This proceeding was incumbent on all guests,—high and low alike,—and was intended to inculcate humility. The order of precedence having been mutually agreed upon while resting in the Machiai, the guests one by one will enter noiselessly and take their seats, first making obeisance to the picture or flower arrangement on the Tokonoma.

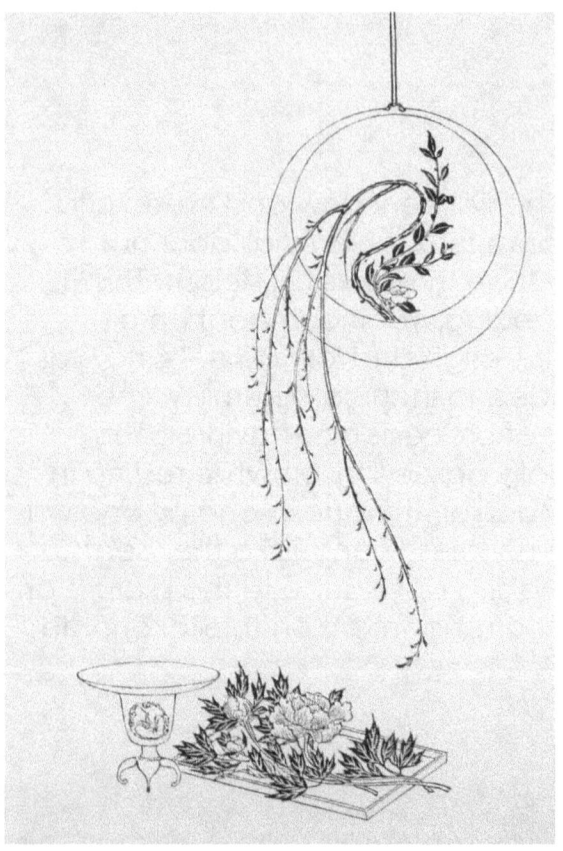

Suspended double arrangement of willow
and camellia in crescent shaped vessel.
Peony flowers and standing vase ready for
arranging below.

The host will not enter the room until all the guests have seated themselves and quiet reigns with nothing to break the silence save the note of the boiling water in the iron kettle. The kettle sings well, for pieces of iron are so arranged in the bottom as to produce a peculiar melody in which one may hear the echoes of a cataract muffled by clouds, of a distant sea breaking among the rocks, a rainstorm sweeping through a bamboo forest, or of the soughing of pines on some faraway hill.

Even in the daytime the light in the room is subdued, for the low eaves of the slanting roof admit but few of the sun's rays. Everything is sober in tint from the ceiling to the floor; the guests themselves have carefully chosen garments of unobtrusive colors. The mellowness of age is over all, everything suggestive of recent acquirement being tabooed save only the one note of contrast furnished by the bamboo dipper and the linen napkin, both immaculately white and new.

However faded the tea-room and the tea-equipage may seem, everything is absolutely clean. Not a particle of dust will be found in the darkest corner, for if any exists the host is not a tea-master. One of the first requisites of a tea-master is the knowledge of how to sweep, clean, and wash, for there is an art in cleaning and dusting.

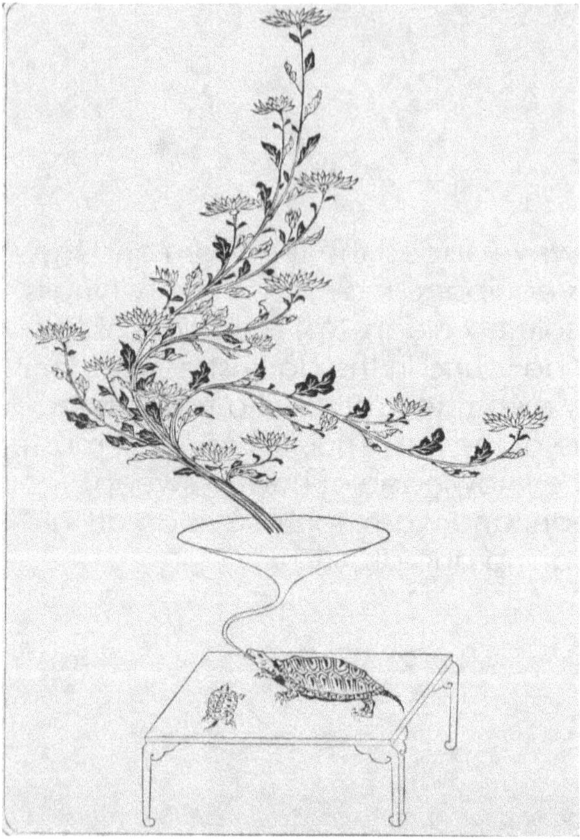

Arrangement of Chrysanthemums with five lines, with seventeen blossoms, in a fancy bronze vase.

The term, Abode of Vacancy, besides conveying the Taoist theory of the all containing, involves the conception of a continued need of change in decorative motives. The tea-room is absolutely empty, except for what may be placed there temporarily to satisfy some aesthetic mood, some special art object is brought in for the occasion, and everything else is selected and arranged to enhance the beauty of the principal theme.

Arrangement of Fitnkia ovata (Giboshi),
a large-leaved water-plant, in an
arrangement of seven leaves.

The Sukiya consists of the tea-room proper, designed to accommodate not more than five persons, a number suggestive of the saying "more than the Graces and less than the Muses," an anteroom (Midsuya) where the tea utensils are washed and arranged before being brought in, a portico (Machiai) in which the guests wait until they receive the summons to enter the tea-room, and a garden path (the Roji) which connects the Machiai with the tea-room.

Arrangement of pine and plum in a vase
made of natural bamboo. The three
forming the floral triad called sho-chiku-bai.

The Roji, the garden path which leads from the Machiai to the tea-room signified the, first stage of meditation,—the passage into self-illumination. The Roji was intended to break connection with the outside world, and to produce a fresh sensation conducive to the full enjoyment of aestheticism in the tea-room itself.

One cannot listen to different pieces of music at the same time, a real comprehension of the beautiful being possible only through concentration upon some central motive. Thus it will be seen that the system of decoration in our tea-rooms is opposed to that which obtains in the West, where the interior of a house is often converted into a museum.

In the tea-room the fear of repetition is a constant presence. The various objects for the decoration of a room should be so selected that no color or design shall be repeated.

マ
ツ

Ikebana pine arrangement.

The dynamic nature of their philosophy laid more stress upon the process through which perfection was sought than upon perfection itself. True beauty could be discovered only by one who mentally completed the incomplete. The virility of life and art lay in its possibilities for growth. In the tea-room it is left for each guest in imagination to complete the total effect in relation to himself.

Ikebana plum and pine arrangement.

The "Abode of the Unsymmetrical" suggests another phase of our decorative scheme.

Japanese Interior. Arrangement of spring flowers.

In the sixteenth century the tea-room afforded a welcome respite from labor to the fierce warriors and statesmen engaged in the unification and reconstruction of Japan. In the seventeenth century, after the strict formalism of the Tokugawa rule had been developed, it offered the only opportunity possible for the free communion of artistic spirits. Before a great work of art there was no distinction between daimyo, samurai, and commoner. Nowadays industrialism is making true refinement more and more difficult all the world over. Do we not need the tearoom more than ever?

The whole ideal of Teaism is a result of
this Zen conception of greatness in the
smallest incidents of life.

The tea-master deems his duty ended with the selection of the flowers, and leaves them to tell their own story. Entering a tearoom in late winter, you may see a slender spray of wild cherries in combination with a budding camellia; it is an echo of departing winter coupled with the prophecy of spring. Again, if you go into a noon-tea on some irritatingly hot summer day, you may discover in the darkened coolness of the Tokonoma a single lily in a hanging vase; dripping with dew, it seems to smile at the foolishness of life.

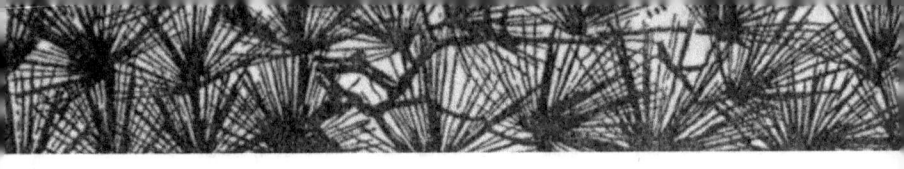

Japanese Interior. Arrangement of summer flowers.

The primeval man in offering the
first garland to his maiden thereby
transcended the brute. He became
human in thus rising above the crude
necessities of nature.

ムメ、カレキク

Ikebana plum arrangement.

A flower arrangement by a tea-master loses its significance if removed from the place for which it was originally intended, for its lines and proportions have been specially worked out with a view to its surroundings.

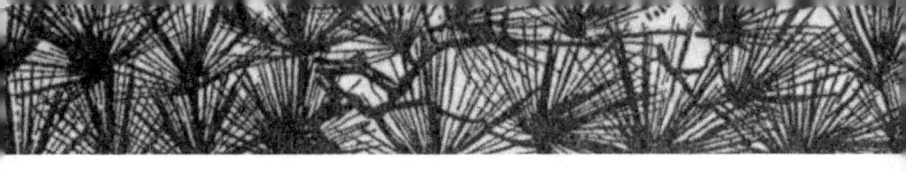

Japanese Interior. Lady arranging lotus flowers.

Dripping water from a flower vase
need not be wiped away, for it may be
suggestive of dew and coolness.

Arranging flowers from "Ikebana no tebiki".

In joy or sadness, flowers are our constant friends. We eat, drink, sing, dance, and flirt with them. We wed and christen with flowers. We dare not die without them. We have worshipped with the lily, we have meditated with the lotus, we have charged in battle array with the rose and the chrysanthemum.

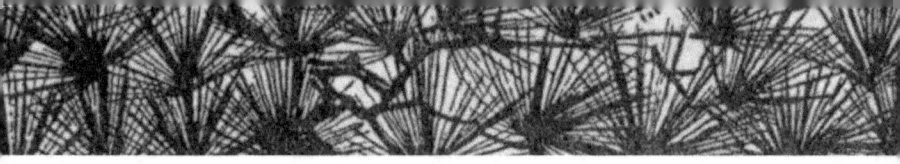

The art of life lies in a constant readjustment to our surroundings. Taoism accepts the mundane as it is and, unlike the Confucians and the Buddhists, tries to find beauty in our world of woe and worry. The Sung allegory of the Three Vinegar Tasters explains admirably the trend of the three doctrines. Sakyamuni, Confucius, and Laotse once stood before a jar of vinegar—the emblem of life—and each dipped in his finger to taste the brew. The matter of-fact Confucius found it sour, the Buddha called it bitter, and Laotse pronounced it sweet.

Our finite nature, the power of tradition and conventionality, as well as our hereditary instincts, restrict the scope of our capacity for artistic enjoyment. Our very individuality establishes in one sense a limit to our understanding; and our aesthetic personality seeks its own affinities in the creations of the past.

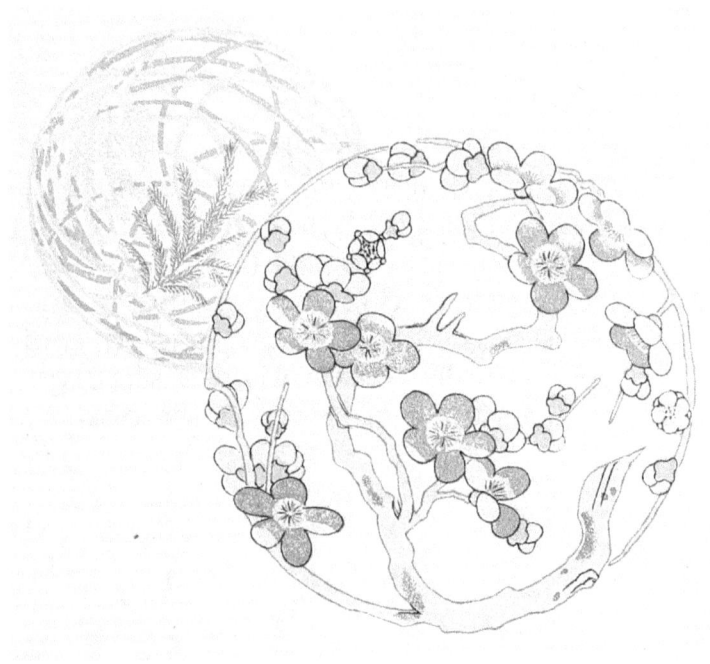

Why were the flowers born so beautiful and yet so hapless? Insects can sting, and even the meekest of beasts will fight when brought to bay. The birds whose plumage is sought to deck some bonnet can fly from its pursuer, the furred animal whose coat you covet for your own may hide at your approach.

Japanese tea room with an arrangement of autumn flowers.

In such instances we see the full significance of the Flower Sacrifice. Perhaps the flowers appreciate the full significance of it. They are not cowards, like men. Some flowers glory in death — certainly the Japanese cherry blossoms do, as they freely surrender themselves to the winds. Anyone who has stood before the fragrant avalanche at Yoshino or Arashiyama must have realized this. For a moment they hover like bejeweled clouds and dance above the crystal streams; then, as they sail away on the laughing waters, they seem to say: "Farewell, O Spring! We are on to Eternity."

Typical Woman of the Ukio-ye School. Japanese Art by Sadakichi Hartmann.

It has been said that man at ten is an animal, at twenty a lunatic, at thirty a failure, at forty a fraud, and at fifty a criminal. Perhaps he becomes a criminal because he has never ceased to be an animal. Nothing is real to us but hunger, nothing sacred except our own desires. Shrine after shrine has crumbled before our eyes; but one altar forever is preserved, that whereon we burn incense to the supreme idol,— ourselves. Our god is great, and money is his Prophet! We devastate nature in order to make sacrifice to him. We boast that we have conquered Matter and forget that it is Matter that has enslaved us.

Perhaps I betray my own ignorance of the Tea Cult by being so outspoken. Its very spirit of politeness exacts that you say what you are expected to say, and no more. But I am not to be a polite Teaist. So much harm has been done already by the mutual misunderstanding of the New World and the Old that one need not apologize for contributing his tithe to the furtherance of a better understanding.

No student of Japanese culture could ever ignore its presence. It [Teaism] has permeated the elegance of noble boudoirs, and entered the abode of the humble. Our peasants have learned to arrange flowers, our meanest labourer to offer his salutation to the rocks and waters.